D0906958

PORSCHE
911 CARRERA
BY EMILY ROSE OACHS

BELLWETHER MEDIA • MINNEAPOLIS, MN

TM

Are you ready to take it to the extreme?
Torque books thrust you into the action-packed world
of sports, vehicles, mystery, and adventure. These books may
include dirt, smoke, fire, and dangerous stunts.
WARNING : read at your own risk.

This edition first published in 2018 by Bellwether Media, Inc.

No part of this publication may be reproduced in whole or in part without written permission of the publisher. For information regarding permission, write to Bellwether Media, Inc., Attention: Permissions Department, 5357 Penn Avenue South, Minneapolis, MN 55419.

Library of Congress Cataloging-in-Publication Data

Names: Oachs, Emily Rose, author.
Title: Porsche 911 Carrera / by Emily Rose Oachs.
Description: Minneapolis, MN : Bellwether Media, Inc., 2018. | Series:
   Torque: Car Crazy | Includes bibliographical references and index. |
   Audience: Ages 7-12.
Identifiers: LCCN 2017031295 (print) | LCCN 2017032234 (ebook) | ISBN 9781626177796
   (hardcover : alk. paper) | ISBN 9781681034843 (ebook)
Subjects: LCSH: Porsche 911 automobile–Juvenile literature.
Classification: LCC TL215.P75 (ebook) | LCC TL215.P75 O23 2018 (print) | DDC
   629.222/2–dc23
LC record available at https://lccn.loc.gov/2017031295

Editor: Betsy Rathburn   Designer: Josh Brink

Printed in the United States of America, North Mankato, MN.

TABLE OF CONTENTS

SPEED AND STYLE 8

THE HISTORY OF PORSCHE 12

PORSCHE 911 CARRERA 14

TECHNOLOGY AND GEAR 20

TODAY AND THE FUTURE 22

GLOSSARY 23

TO LEARN MORE 24

INDEX ....

SPEED AND STYLE

A driver unlocks the door to his Porsche 911 Carrera. Then, he steps inside. He settles into his brand-new sports car.

The driver turns the key, and the engine hums. He presses his foot to the gas pedal, and the car bursts forward.

All eyes are on the 911 Carrera as it whizzes down the road. The car's smooth lines and classy style do not disappoint.

The driver rounds a corner, and the car zooms out of sight!

THE HISTORY OF PORSCHE

Ferdinand Porsche

In the early 1900s, Ferdinand Porsche introduced his record-breaking electric car. Soon, he was known around the world for his skill. He later worked on race cars for top companies in Germany.

In 1931, Ferdinand and his son started their own company. The company introduced its first car, the Porsche 356, in 1948.

RACING CHAMPS!

PORSCHE PRODUCED RACING CHAMPIONS FROM THE VERY BEGINNING. THE PORSCHE 356 WON ITS FIRST RACE JUST WEEKS AFTER IT WAS INTRODUCED.

Porsche 356

Throughout the 1950s, Porsche vehicles sped to victory in many racing events. They impressed car lovers around the world!

1956 24 Hours of Le Mans race

MOVIE STAR CARS

OVER THE YEARS, PORSCHE VEHICLES HAVE BEEN FEATURED IN MANY MOVIES. IN 2006, THE MOVIE *CARS* FEATURED A 911 CARRERA CHARACTER NAMED SALLY CARRERA!

Today, Porsche is famous for both its racing success and its wide range of **luxury** vehicles. Its lineup includes sports cars and SUVs. These vehicles bring Porsche's racing spirit to everyday driving!

PORSCHE 911 CARRERA

The first Porsche 911 was introduced in 1964. It soon became one of the world's most recognized sports cars. Many other 911 styles have been made since then.

In the 1970s, the first 911 Carrera was introduced. It was built to race! The car can be either a **coupe** or a **convertible**. Each has the luxury and power of the original.

coupe

convertible

NAMED *FOR DANGER*

PORSCHE NAMED THE 911 CARRERA AFTER THE CARRERA PANAMERICANA. THIS RACE CROSSED THOUSANDS OF MILES OF MEXICO. IT WAS SO DANGEROUS THAT IT ONLY TOOK PLACE FIVE TIMES.

Porsche 911 SC

TECHNOLOGY AND GEAR

The Porsche 911 Carrera's power comes from its **flat-6 engine**. The engine sits behind the car's second row of seats. **Turbochargers** push it to 370 horsepower.

flat-6 engine

HELPFUL VENTS

VENTS ON THE FRONT OF THE CAR OPEN AND CLOSE TO IMPROVE PERFORMANCE. WHEN OPEN, THE VENTS DRAW COOL AIR TO THE ENGINE. WHEN THE VENTS ARE CLOSED, THE CAR IS MORE AERODYNAMIC.

The car's body is low and wide. Designers chose this **aerodynamic** shape for the racetrack. A **spoiler** pops up when the car travels at high speeds. It keeps the car steady.

Inside, top-of-the-line technology makes the car feel comfortable and modern. **Sensors** control the temperature on their own.

A wide touch screen sits on the dashboard. From it, the driver can control the stereo or **navigation**. An **app** tracks and logs the car's performance. This allows the driver to keep the information close.

touch screen

vents

Porsche built the 911 Carrera to combine **sustainability** and performance. Recyclable plastic, **aluminum**, and steel are used to make the body. These materials make the car lightweight yet strong. The lighter body allows the sports car to burn less fuel while traveling.

2017 PORSCHE 911 CARRERA SPECIFICATIONS

CAR STYLE	COUPE OR CONVERTIBLE
ENGINE	3.0L FLAT-6
TOP SPEED	183 MILES (295 KILOMETERS) PER HOUR
0 - 60 TIME	4.4 SECONDS
HORSEPOWER	370 HP (276 KILOWATTS) @ 6,500 RPM
CURB WEIGHT	3,153 POUNDS (1,430 KILOGRAMS)
WIDTH	71.2 INCHES (181 CENTIMETERS)
LENGTH	177.1 INCHES (450 CENTIMETERS)
HEIGHT	50.9 INCHES (129 CENTIMETERS)
WHEEL SIZE	19 INCHES (48 CENTIMETERS)
COST	STARTS AT $91,100

TODAY AND THE FUTURE

Today, Porsche continues to improve the 911 Carrera. Fans never have to wait long to see the latest version.

As new changes are introduced, the car will only get better. Whether rounding a curve or racing down a **straightaway**, the 911 Carrera brings comfort and speed wherever it goes!

HOW TO SPOT A PORSCHE 911 CARRERA

ROUND HEADLIGHTS

BACK VENTS

SLOPING ROOFLINE

GLOSSARY

aerodynamic—having a shape that can move through the air quickly

aluminum—a strong, lightweight metal

app—a small, specialized program downloaded onto a smartphone or other mobile device

convertible—a car with a folding or soft roof

coupe—a car with a hard roof and two doors

flat-6 engine—an engine with six cylinders arranged in two rows of three and laid flat

luxury—expensive and offering great comfort

navigation—a car system that provides maps and directions to get around

sensors—devices that help a car respond to changes in driving conditions

spoiler—a part on the back of the car that helps the car grip the road

straightaway—the straight parts of a track

sustainability—the use of environment-friendly materials that can be recycled

rbochargers—parts that increase a car's horsepower

TO LEARN MORE

AT THE LIBRARY

Crane, Cody. *Race Cars.* New York, N.Y.: Children's Press, 2018.

Cruz, Calvin. *Porsche 918 Spyder.* Minneapolis, Minn.: Bellwether Media, 2016.

Piddock, Charles. *Porsche 911.* Vero Beach, Fla.: Rourke Educational Media, 2016.

ON THE WEB

Learning more about the Porsche 911 Carrera is as easy as 1, 2, 3.

1. Go to www.factsurfer.com.

2. Enter "Porsche 911 Carrera" into the search box.

3. Click the "Surf" button and you will see a list of related web sites.

With factsurfer.com, finding more information is just a click away.

INDEX

aerodynamic, 15

app, 16

body, 12, 15, 18

Carrera Panamericana, 13

Cars (movie), 11

comfort, 16, 20

company, 9, 10,
    11, 13, 18, 20

electric car, 8

engine, 4, 14, 15

Germany, 8

history, 8, 9, 10, 11, 12

how to spot, 21

interior, 16

models, 9, 11, 13

name, 13

navigation, 16

Porsche, Ferdinand, 8, 9

racing, 9, 10, 11,
    12, 13, 15, 20

sensors, 16

specifications, 19

speed, 15, 20

spoiler, 15

sustainability, 18

technology, 16

touch screen, 16

turbochargers, 14

vents, 15, 17, 21